IT'S TIME TO STOP

To Marlene

It's a great pleasure, my intention is something inside assists you to a better life.

8/8/13

IT'S TIME TO STOP
IT'S TIME TO STOP
IT'S TIME TO STOP
IT'S TIME TO STOP
IT'S TIME TO STOP
IT'S TIME TO STOP
IT'S TIME TO STOP
IT'S TIME TO STOP
IT'S TIME TO STOP
IT'S TIME TO STOP
IT'S TIME TO STOP
IT'S TIME TO STOP
IT'S TIME TO STOP
IT'S TIME TO STOP
IT'S TIME TO STOP

Stanley W. Allen

©CARMAA PUBLISHING
A MARY BOOK

Copyright © 2009 by CARMAA Publishing, LLC. All rights reserved.

Two Harbors Press
212 3rd Avenue North, Suite 570
Minneapolis, MN 55401
612.455.2293
www.TwoHarborsPress.com

All rights reserved. No part of this book may be reproduced or utilized in any form or by means, electronic or mechanical, including photocopying, recording or by and information storage or retrieval system without the permission in writing from the writer of this publication.

ISBN - 978-1-935097-29-7
ISBN - 1-935097-29-6
LCCN - 2008911000

Book sales for North America and international:
Itasca Books, 3501 Highway 100 South, Suite 220
Minneapolis, MN 55416
Phone: 952.345.4488 (toll free 1.800.901.3480)
Fax: 952.920.0541; email to orders@itascabooks.com

Typeset by Sophie Chi
Edited by T. V. Marshall
Cover Design by Michael Tinglin
Website Design by Shine Interactive Design Agency, Plano Texas

Distributed in the United States and Canada by CARMAA Publishing LLC

A MARY BOOK

Dedicated in Memory to
Mr. & Mrs. Carl Allen Sr.

"Reading is very important to make it in this world. You must read something new everyday. But remember that if you can't read too well, that does not mean that you can't live a nice life. Reading only helps you to do it better."

Carl Sr.

"Dreams are something that you need to take a good look at every now and then, especially if you can remember them. Many times dreams are there for you to make them real in your life, whether that is to keep you safe or to do something. Never be afraid of dreams, sometimes that's God's way of talking to you."

Mary

You are never forgotten. You and your words, love and your love for life will always live in my heart forever.

Buddy

ACKNOWLEDGMENTS

The names of people who have come into my life in support of this project are too numerous to write down. Many have come in a variety of ways, all teaching me something new, whether that is a new way of believing in me or giving me the understanding that I can do it.

To everyone who feels that their name should be included in this book, you are included; you are included in the words that are printed on each page. You are included with every thought, all the effort, the long, long hours it took to complete this project, and the labor it involved. Your names are written.

Thanks to each of you, you know who you are. If I must include any names they would be:
To my grandparents, who loved me when others would not.
To Eden Michelle, who stuck by me in those moments.
To "Goober" – Thanks.
To Mickey for his visions and know how.
To my editor, T., who *would not reach out and touch me.* :-)

To you, the reader of this book, whom I know will gain knowledge to live life to the fullest.

Thanks.

"When real people come into our lives, they become real friends, who become real love ones, who become real people, who become real support, and who become people that you learn to respect and cherish."

-Stanley W. Allen

MY METHODOLOGY

If you are sitting down in the comfort of your place of residence, riding the bus, sitting in your office, or on your lunch break at the park, and you are reading this little book, you are fortunate to be on the road to living life to the fullest. You may have been intrigued by the cover, or maybe the mere title caught your attention. At some point, you decided that you needed to have this book in your possession. You are right! You NEED this book. I wrote this book with the intention to reach every individual—the rich, the poor, the depressed, the married, the unmarried, the educated, and the individuals who think that they are not too well educated—everyone. It does not matter who you are. This book is for you.

The contents are just as it says on the cover: *It's Time to Stop!* You may be asking yourself, "Stop what?" The following pages will assist you in discovering exactly what you need to stop doing or not doing to live life to the fullest. Like you, I, too, want to live life to the fullest. This was a personal project of mine to seek deep within my soul and find things that would assist me in living life to the fullest. Allow me to explain what I mean when I say "living life to the fullest." Just like every other person, I grew up being conditioned to follow the way of life and have the same beliefs, principles, and ethics of my family. I was conditioned to believe and act a certain way. Not all of it was wrong. Nor was all of it for me. As I matured, I began to see life in a different way. I have seen things differently than the ways they were presented to me. I have great respect for those who came before me. Most, if not all, of them provided me and others with great strength, wisdom, and love. But as I matured, I felt restricted — restricted in thought, mind, body, and soul. I needed more. I wanted more; therefore, I sought to seek deep within myself to find the answers.

Through searching my inner being, I found that there were a variety of things that I, too, needed to stop. I needed to stop the way I was thinking. I needed to stop the way I was behaving about certain things in my life. I made a lot of bad decisions. I have since learned that each mistake was not really merely a mistake. It was an opportunity for me to stop and find a way not to make the same mistake again.

As I began my mission of writing the things I needed to stop, I had no idea that it would involve me sharing them with others. I was excited and wanted others I knew to live life to the fullest, also. Although I received the encouragement of others who said that I should write a book about my journey, my first thought was that I could never do that. That led me to begin a list. The first item that I wrote was to stop doubting. And, guess what? I did. You will see the proof of that in this book. My intention was to write in simple terms. I wanted to write something that others could understand—not a bunch of words on a page, but something that would help individuals to begin living life to the fullest.

This book was not intended to focus on one subject, as it could have been. Our lives are not centered on just one subject or dilemma. We, as people, have myriad dilemmas that plague us, some more important than others. Yes, on subjects such as hatred, or not loving oneself, or low self-esteem, it can affect many of us, but not all of us are affected by the subject. Although a single subject can affect a great number of people, everyone will not respond the same way. We all have different thoughts, and although some may share the same dilemma, each person will see it differently.

As stated throughout this book, it is intended for all. It does look at a variety of issues that may make people, all people, at some time in their lives look inside themselves and say, "I need to stop behaving or thinking like this and change for myself." While reading this book, you may not find an item that you feel may be for you, but you may know someone else who needs to read this book. Pass it on.

Everyone deserves the best. Many of us do not believe that we deserve anything. You need to stop and know that you can do anything your heart desires. You can have anything your mind can conceive. You must first believe that you can, know that you are worthy of it, and know that your source, the Universal Provider of all, has intended it for you. Before I continue, allow me to clear something up. When I say "Universal Provider," I'm talking about God, Jehovah, Ali, Buddha, whomever or whatever you believe is the entity who is above all mankind. This is not a religious overtone. It is just a fact for me. I call the higher source "Universal Provider." The Provider has provided the air that we breathe, the water that we drink, the sun, and the moon for every person who lives on this earth. The Provider gives all this to you, them, they, and me—everyone. Now that that is understood, let's continue.

"Life as we know it today." Wow! What a statement. The 21st century has come with many challenges. In the times that we live, at this moment, there are some people who are living their lives on pins and needles, wondering what could be next. Some are living scared out of their minds wondering, "How in the hell am I going to make it? How are my children going to make it? How am I going to keep this house and car? What's going to happen to my credit? Am I going to make it without my spouse should I lose him or her?"

The world today seems as if it is moving faster and faster than ever before. Or has it always been moving at the same pace, and we were just not receptive enough of its axes? Or is it that our minds have been moving at a different vibrational level? My answer to the question: I believe the earth moves at the same pace as it always has; it's just that we, as people, are moving faster than the earth *(only in our minds)*. Let me explain. Man's progression has allowed us to travel in space and create a space station. I have asked for years and have not heard anyone give me a real, substantial explanation as to why we are in space building a space station. Maybe you may know, or I may not be asking the right people. For man to build or even think that he could and would build something in the sky can be a little profound for the average mind such as mine.

Let's play a history game. Go back with me to the 1500s. No, let's go back even further, say 135 B.C. What do you think people of that time were thinking? I'll bet my family's farm and money *(if they had any now)* that people of that era had no idea what stairs, cars, televisions, stoves, toothbrushes, combs, or brushes were. A space station in the sky? Give me a break. Travel with me from 135 B.C. through history to a period in time when man figured out that he could create a stove to cook with, the car, and the television— something to look at other than his spouse. Was the earth moving faster at each of those times, or was it man thinking more? Continue to travel through history with me to a time when man came up with the invention of the airplane. Was the earth moving faster, or was man thinking more? I think you get the picture.

Well, come back with me to today's time, here in 2008 A.D. We have—guess what? A space station in the sky, for what purpose, as stated before, I really do not know. Now, as I said at the beginning of this chapter, I believe that the earth is moving at the same pace as it always has since its creation, but the progression of man's mind is moving faster. Almost every household in America, and most places throughout the world, has a microwave and uses it for daily cooking. Food is zapped in nanoseconds. Today we have automakers working on better fuel efficiency. There are some vehicles that are running on cooking oil. Automakers are testing cars that can drive without a driver. The list goes on. People are communicating in real time with the Internet all across the world at the same time. The medical industry has moved into warp speed; they are doing things today that were not possible just a few years ago. Doctors can detect defects of a fetus while in the mother's womb. There are machines that can view the inside of a person's body to detect certain illnesses at their beginning stages. Surgeries that once were almost fatal are today done routinely. There are weapons/ machinery that can destroy a million people within minutes. Unmanned planes can fly spying on people and never be detected. Again, the list continues.

I wrote this book to assist, inspire, and motivate individuals to take a minute and **STOP, LOOK, and LISTEN** to what's going on around them—around their environment, their families, their lives, and themselves. If we, as adults, would take time somewhere in our lives to (1) STOP; (2) LOOK; and (3) LISTEN, most of us would be able to make sense of the world that envelops us. Some people have taken the position to just listen to others and allow other people to make sense of what happens in their worlds. There are other people who just accept anything that comes their way. And, for others, they can become so consumed with the elements of money, hate, love, sex, religion, debt, family, possessions, achievements, race, class, and egos that they miss the real purpose of their existence here on Earth. Most people never really have the opportunity to enjoy what life is all about. Life is more than just you. Life is more than just others. Life is more than just what you have in your possession, and life is more than your accomplishments and your degrees. It's about everything. Everything, and everyone, is to be respected, enjoyed, and treasured. For us to do that, sometimes we just need to say to others and to ourselves, **"It's Time To Stop!"**

I want to stress that this book was not intended to be a fix-all, just something to make you, the reader, think about your life and see what can assist you to live life to the fullest.

In this book you will find a few exercises, where there are no right or wrong answers. They are for you to think about the questions to gain a better understanding about that subject, by understanding, it may assist you in living life to the fullest. With that understanding, you may just decide to stop, and, if so, you are on the road to a better life.

Inside this book you will find that not all of the items will be expounded upon. My intention was to allow you, the reader, to think about what it means to you. The items that were expounded upon were done so at random, understanding that not every item is for everyone, but everyone can stop something to live life to the fullest. The intention of this book was to inspire, motivate, and encourage you

Take a browse through this book and find something that you may need to stop. There's something that you may need to change. There's something that you need to start doing so that you can become able to enjoy life to the fullest. The Universal Provider has already thought about this long before you were an embryo—that life can be, and is, fun, rich, full, pleasant, and so much more. You just need to stop the wheels of negative motion and change what you see, think, and do to appreciate life more than you do today. You were created to be the best. If you allow yourself to be consumed with the elements, the pitfalls, the material things, and, most importantly, the things that hold no value at all, you can, and most often will, miss out on the very important things that life has to offer. It may take a while for some to understand this concept. For others, you get the picture. If we do not take time to say to others and ourselves that **"It's Time to Stop,"** life will move on and, before you know it, is over in just a moment.

While browsing through this book, if you find that none of the items in this list applies to you in your current situation, stop. Look deep inside your soul and read this book again. I'm sure you will find one, maybe even two, or three items that you need to stop doing. If after soul searching and reading this book twice, you can't find anything that applies to you, pass it on to someone else you feel may be in need of living life to the fullest. You have achieved your goal. Congratulations. Go forth and LIVE! However, if you see things you need to stop in this book, stop and take the time to work through them. Read this book again and again. Use this book as a tool to help you build a better you.

Let's go and see together what we can STOP in our lives in order for us to…

"LIVE LIFE TO THE FULLEST"

CHAPTER I

WHO AM I?

1. IT'S TIME TO STOP: Living Without Recognizing That A Creator Exists.
2. IT'S TIME TO STOP: Living In Fear.
3. IT'S TIME TO STOP: Not Remembering Where You Come From.
4. IT'S TIME TO STOP: Being Unforgiving.
5. IT'S TIME TO STOP: Being Uncreative.
6. IT'S TIME TO STOP: **Not Knowing Who You Are.**

Who are you? Do you really know who you are? No, I do not mean the name that your parents or family members gave to you at birth. I'm not speaking about your age or your gender. I am not speaking about your family's heritage (a Vanderbilt, Trump, Hilton, or the child of the president's *family's wealth*).

I am not speaking about your accomplishments/ achievements or your religion. Well, what do I mean? Most people live almost their entire lives not knowing who they truly are. Most can tell you in minutes who other people are! They know someone else's character or behavior — if that person is a lazy person, a hateful person, or a person who is a go-getter. When the question comes to defining one's self, many of us draw a blank. It becomes very difficult to describe who we really are as individuals. Most people spend countless amounts of energy knowing other people, but not themselves. Many of us have been taught that what we have in our possessions is who we are. How much money we have in the bank and/or how many achievements we have accumulated really defines us. But, in essence, that does not define us. It only describes what we can do, rather than who we truly are. Who we are in our eyes — it is the fiber, our soul. That is how I describe who I am.

- Soul
- Body
- Mind
- Spirit

Now, we can put it in any order, but just think about this for a moment. Do you really know your soul? What moves you or what drives you? Are you really in touch with your soul? Many will say that I have a religious side of me that defines my soul. I believe in God and all of its manifesting: Judaism, Christianity, Islam, or Buddhism. The soul is defined as "the embodiment, personification, the intensity of emotion and expression." It is a person's spiritual, emotional, and moral nature. Do you really know your soul and how it acts?

Do you really know your body? Can you say that you know when your body is talking to you? Do you listen for warning signs? Do you spend time examining your body to know every mark? Do you accept the body that you were given? Most people have no clue in understanding their bodies and only concern themselves when something is wrong or something happens that causes them to take notice.

Are you in control of your mind? Do you allow others to make decisions for you? Most of us have been taught to listen and follow instructions. We listen for what others think about any situation; and, if we agree with their thoughts about a particular situation, we are more inclined to stay with their thoughts. If we disagree, most often than not, we will seek others for their opinions. In most cases, we will continue to seek opinions until we become satisfied. Are you one of those people who is able to think independently and not be influenced by others? If we would take the time to know our own minds and be comfortable with ourselves, we would know that what we think about becomes what we do and say.

Our spirits are totally different, and yet the same as our souls. They do concern themselves with feelings and emotions. I believe that the spirit is that part of us that guides us, protects us from danger and oftentimes from the unforeseen things. I also believe that the spirit is what was breathed into man to make him a living soul. You may not agree with that statement, but this is my methodology. Do you fully understand your spirit? When you have an understanding of your Soul, your Body, your Mind, and your Spirit, you will definitely know who you are.

Here is one way to get started and find out if you really know yourself. You may be asking, "Why would I not know myself? I have been with myself from the beginning. I know what I will do and what I will not do." Well, you are correct that you may know what you will and will not do, but that is what you know by being taught as a child; you were taught that this or that is right or wrong. Open your mind, and go with me for a minute. You will be in control of your thoughts, and you will have the final say. Let's take this little test:

You must follow the instructions. You must answer truthfully. No one will know if you are not being truthful but you. Many people will lie to themselves because they are unsure of who they are. Many people think that if they just say to themselves that something is not what they think it is, then it isn't. But, in actuality, it just may be true, and you may be denying the truth. Self knows the truth; many people just cannot accept the truth. So be in agreement with yourself, and you will live a lot better.

Here are the instructions: This test will take three minutes. It must be taken without the assistance of anyone. You must not think about the questions before taking this test. Below, complete the twenty-four lines by completing the statement "I Am…" with one word. Please remember that you have only three minutes for the entire test. Before you begin, set a timer for three minutes. Let's take the test:

Who Am I?   No, Really Who Am I?
Example: I am **Man** / **Strong** / **Healthy**

1. I Am _____   I Am _____
2. I Am _____   I Am _____
3. I Am _____   I Am _____
4. I Am _____   I Am _____
5. I Am _____   I Am _____
6. I Am _____   I Am _____
7. I Am _____   I Am _____
8. I Am _____   I Am _____
9. I Am _____   I Am _____
10. I Am _____   I Am _____
11. I Am _____   I Am _____
12. I Am _____   I Am _____

Number of Completed Lines: _____
Number of Incomplete Lines: _____
Now, take a look at how many lines you have

completed, and ask yourself, "Do I know who I am?" Take a moment and relax. As you think about who you are, smile and be happy. Think about the things that you want to change. You can change those things.

7. IT'S TIME TO STOP: Being Unconcerned.
8. IT'S TIME TO STOP: Allowing Others To Speak For You.
9. IT'S TIME TO STOP: Being What Others Want You To Be.
10. IT'S TIME TO STOP: **Believing That You Are Unsuccessful.**

Most of us have been taught that being a doctor, lawyer, or businessman/woman are the only things that make us successful. That is one of the most outrageous things that we could ever be told. Yes, it is true that those professions are great, and, for the most part, they do make a great deal of money. There are so many other professions that are equally important.

While I was in school, I had almost every job imaginable, just to have a little money in my pocket. I worked making buttons. I pulled this lever up and down to make plastic and metal buttons all day. It was "boring," of course, and I quit after two days. Although the business was boring to me, the owner of that business was very successful. He had orders coming in from everywhere. I once had a job cleaning small businesses, but I was fired from that job. I fell asleep too many times. The owner of that business had a big house and a fancy car; he, too, was very successful. I also had a job stocking shelves at a local grocery store. Well, you know the story ends in me being fired. I let my friends take whatever they wanted. Of course, it was just things they needed, like toilet paper, gum, candy, chips, bread, milk, etc. So, I was again fired for not protecting the stores merchandise.

The most exciting job I had was being a trash collector. Yes, I said *trash man* was the coolest job I ever had while in school. Although it was a very dirty and smelly job, I made a lot of money; I had the hours I needed; and I worked full time and went to school full time. I only picked up residential trash for about a month, but for the next three years I drove the truck picking up commercial trash. It was easy and allowed me to see what people did to make them successful. I met people from all walks of life. I was fired from that job, too, because I had a small accident in the truck. I hit a tree limb, and it fell on someone's car, but I kept driving and did not stop. I knew something happened, but I did not know the full extent. So, I lost the job for failing to stop at the scene of an accident. Now, you may say that I sure was fired a lot. Yes, maybe that makes me a very successful fired person. I'm here to tell you that you can be successful at anything you desire to do and be. Well, if you only knew that the trash business is a multibillion dollar business. It is something that everyone needs, to have your trash taken away.

Never allow anyone to degrade you because you pick up trash, work at McDonald's™, paint cars, work in the sewer, dig ditches, fix computers, or mow lawns for a living. The Creator has provided each and every one of us with tools that will not just make the world go round, but also take care of you. You just need to know who and what you are and do it. Just do it. You are successful if you are a stay-at-home mom, if that's what you do. Being a full-time mom is no joke. Whether you have a house of four or a house of twelve, it's all the same. It takes skills to do it effectively. Again, you are successful if you are doing anything that does not hurt others.

CHAPTER II

FREE YOUR MIND

11. IT'S TIME TO STOP: Being A Follower And Not Thinking Independently.
12. IT'S TIME TO STOP: Allowing Others To Decide Your Future.
13. IT'S TIME TO STOP: Being A Racist.
14. IT'S TIME TO STOP: Believing Everything You Hear.
15. IT'S TIME TO STOP: Not Using Your Mind.
16. IT'S TIME TO STOP: Watching Too Much Television.
17. IT'S TIME TO STOP: **Worrying What Others Think About You.**

How you feel about yourself is more important than what others think of you. If you do not believe in yourself, love yourself, respect yourself, others will never truly believe in you or respect you. Most people are always looking to find themselves in others. People in our society place a great deal of time and money in concerning themselves about what others think. We see it in the movies, on television, sports, competitions, pageants, and the list continues. Allow me to make this simple and plain: The most important thing you can ever do is to believe in yourself and know that you are not responsible for what others think. You trust you, love you, be you, and take care of you. Here is a quote that I learned as a child: "Whatever you love you cannot destroy." Stop worrying what others think of you and live for you.

CHAPTER III

DESTROYING YOURSELF

18. IT'S TIME TO STOP: Being Careless.
19. IT'S TIME TO STOP: Being Irresponsible.
20. IT'S TIME TO STOP: Being Mad.
21. IT'S TIME TO STOP: Being Negative All The DAMN Time.
22. IT'S TIME TO STOP: **Being Offended.**

If you have ever been offended by someone who said something or did something to you, then you know what it feels like to be offended. A joke can be offensive. A comment about your clothes may be offensive. The lack of a smile from someone who passes you in a hallway can be offensive. Your mom or dad not recognize something that you feel is important to you can be offensive. The list continues. Everyday, each one of us is offended by someone or something. Most people are offended by what others think and say about them, but the behaviors of others should never be a question for how one lives their life. I know that it is easier than said than done.

The thoughts of others should not render us powerless or cause our dreams and hopes to fade away. We must understand that sometimes when we are offended it takes something from us; it takes our drive away, our desire, and, most importantly, our will to continue our goals. Pleasing others is what we have been taught. We have been taught to respect our parents, our family, our job, law enforcement, religious leaders, etc. Now, I am not advocating that we should not respect those who are in authority. We can easily be offended by what these entities think about us. For the most part, most of us learn to respect and reply to the responses of others. And when we let them down, we lose a part of ourselves. It is time to stop allowing ourselves to be offended.

Yes, one can offend himself or herself. If you know who and what you are and understand your vision, offending yourself does not become a self-defeating issue. One thing you must know is that living a superficial existence is one way to offend yourself. What do I mean by superficial? Being superficial is living in a manner you know does not represent the real you, the you that many others may not know. It is living the life that makes others believe that you have it all together—everything in your life is great: your job, your relationships, your spirituality, your finances, etc. It is knowing that behind closed doors that could be the furthest from the truth. Only you know that things are really going well in your life and that it may be time to stop living a lie. Some may need to have better relationships with their families, but we will often make it appear that our relationships are well. Should someone from the outside say something about our relationships that disagrees with what we want them to know? We become offended; we will begin to experience pain, feel insulted, slighted, etc. I can't say it any simpler that that. It's Time To Stop! Most of our lives are spent pleasing someone else. We are often afraid of letting others know how we feel or what we care about. You must be unadulterated in everything that you do. Just be you. People will never agree on everything, and, if so, that would be very boring. Someone somewhere will see things much differently than you. Keep your goals at the top of your thought process, and allow your thoughts to have control of your processes of living. We are what we think; therefore, when one or something comes to take offense against you, you will have the reserve to withstand the test of time.

23. IT'S TIME TO STOP: Being Uncareful.
24. IT'S TIME TO STOP: Carrying Other's Pain.
25. IT'S TIME TO STOP: Cheating Yourself Out of Life.
26. IT'S TIME TO STOP: Creating Your Own Misery.

27. IT'S TIME TO STOP: **Drinking So Much.**

Plain and simple—drinking too much is not a healthy thing that any person should be doing. You know that it is time to stop being a drunk if you have others who depend on you for their livelihood. Your state of drinking may not be a problem for you, but it is affecting the people who surround you.

Alcohol consumption causes a number of changes in your behavior that many of you may not be aware of. Even very low doses can impair your judgment and/or coordination to drive. I think everyone knows that. Low and moderate doses of alcohol can increase the incidence of a variety of aggressive behaviors, including spousal and child abuse. If you are a moderate to an abusive drinker, your impairments are much higher, and your mental functions are severely impaired. It can even cause respiratory depression and even death. Your family deserves much better. For those in the know, alcohol is absorbed from the stomach and intestines into the blood stream. It diffuses quickly into all of the body's tissues, and the blood concentration level indicates its presence. Only about ten percent of the ingested alcohol is directly eliminated through the kidneys and lungs. The rest is metabolized into the liver.

Many may disagree that alcohol is a very powerful depressant to the central nervous system, similar to ether and chloroform. (Ether is a highly flammable liquid compound used as a solvent and anesthetic. Chloroform is a clear heavy liquid used in refrigerants and also as an anesthetic.) Alcohol depresses certain brain cells by interfering with the nerve impulses traveling along the neuronal membrane and by suppressing certain inhibitory behaviors. That is the initial behavioral reaction that may appear to be excitation. That's your emotions that stir up strong feelings. It is what you will see when a drunk person is really angry or out of control.

People who are chronic drinkers are said to be more tolerant to higher levels. The basis of such alcohol tolerance has recently been attributed to an increase in the chemicals called "phospholipids." They lie on the surface of the brain cells. The chronic drinker apparently adapts to this increase and his/her nerve cells to allow a more normal transmission of nerve impulses.

I apologize for being so clinical. When I talk about drugs and alcohol, the therapist comes out of me. If you did not know, drinking can cause liver disease and a multitude of other elements that could end your life. Because we live in the United States, alcohol is legal in all states, and a person is free to drink him/herself to death. For the sake of your loved ones, it may be time to stop drinking so damn much.

Here is a test for you. Write a list of five things you believe are complications and symptoms of alcohol abuse.

1. _____
2. _____
3. _____
4. _____
5. _____

Here is another test for you. List five things that alcohol does for a person.

1. _____
2. _____
3. _____
4. _____
5. _____

Here is one more for you. List five other things (drugs, behaviors, etc.) that a person uses while consuming alcohol.

1. _____
2. _____
3. _____
4. _____
5. _____

I will give you some answers later in the book.

"Change is a part of life. This is one of the biggest lessons in life. Any change or any loss does not have to beat you down so badly that you can't get up again. No matter

where you are in life, no matter what your situation, you can always do something. You always have a choice: either to cope, be content, commit to change, create what you really want, or feel confused and live in a state of crisis. Remember this: When pain and change happens, you will either be mobilized or paralyzed." – Jewel Diamond Taylor

28. IT'S TIME TO STOP: Having Unprotected Sex.
29. IT'S TIME TO STOP: **Not Taking Care of Yourself.**

Learn to take care of your body. Eating the wrong things hurts your body and mind in ways that you could not imagine. Know how your body acts and when changes occur. Take time to stay fit and exercise. Take time to walk. Walking helps your blood flow. Walking, alone, helps you clear your mind. Walk around your block. Go to a safe park. Walk in the mall. Just walk.

Take time to run or jog if you are able. This and other exercises will give you the energy to properly stimulate your mind. Eat what's good for your body; drink plenty of water; and, be grateful when you take care of yourself. This is your body and mind. No one can take care of it but you. Value the temple that you live in, and the temple will value you.

30. IT'S TIME TO STOP: Living As If No One Cares About You.
31. IT'S TIME TO STOP: Living In A Dream Land.

32. IT'S TIME TO STOP: Lying To Yourself.
33. IT'S TIME TO STOP: Selling Your Body.
34. IT'S TIME TO STOP: Selling Your Mind.
35. IT'S TIME TO STOP: Smoking.
36. IT'S TIME TO STOP: Trusting Those You Know Who Are Wrong.
37. IT'S TIME TO STOP: Working So Hard.
38. IT'S TIME TO STOP: **Using Drugs That Control Your Mind.**

Let's talk about this for a moment. For a few years now, this pandemic has affected a great number of people here in America and maybe our entire world. We will explore only two of the top drugs that are affecting so many people from all walks of life. In another book, we may just explore the other variety of drugs that have consumed so many people.

Marijuana

It is the one drug that many say really does not affect you like so many other drugs. It is the one drug that many will attest comes from Mother Earth. Well, yes, you are correct that marijuana comes from Mother Earth, but you are incorrect in stating that it really does not affect you like other drugs and that there is really nothing wrong with smoking a joint. Marijuana is cannabis (the hemp plant or similar to a tropical plant with leaves). This drug has negative effects on your mental stability and your physicality. Several regularly observed physical effects of marijuana are a substantial increase in the heart rate, bloodshot eyes, dry mouth and throat, and sometimes an increase in appetite. With the modern types of marijuana today, the appetite is not as present as it was a decade ago.

When a person uses marijuana, it causes one to be impaired and/or have reduced short-term memory loss and comprehension. The sense of reality becomes altered, such as a sense of time. It reduces the ability to perform tasks that require concentration. Many people believe they are thinking rationally and they can perform things better when they are high, but, in fact, this is not true. Motivation and cognition may be altered, which makes the acquisition of new information difficult. Marijuana can also produce paranoia and psychosis.

In the 1960's many people considered marijuana to be hazard free. Many people saw it as a "soft drug," instead of a hazard. For the past two decades, the THC (tetrahydrocannabinal) content has varied from one to four percent. THC is the mood-altering chemical found in marijuana that delivers the high. If you have ever smoked marijuana back in the day before 1980, you had to smoke a lot more to achieve a real buzz. Today it only takes a puff or two, and you are high as a kite. Today marijuana can contain up to fourteen percent of THC. People who use marijuana are consuming a product at least as potent as the plant's resin, itself. Today's users stay higher longer, and the intoxicating state is much more intense than ever before. The marijuana today has more than four hundred potentially harmful chemicals, and this makes it more difficult to predict its overall effect.

One thing we know is today's marijuana is a very powerful drug. It enables the user to feel high with less than 1/10,000 of an average drink of alcohol. The nerve cells are affected by as little as a billionth of a gram of THC. THC is much weaker than LSD and is four hundred times more potent that the drug mescaline (a hallucinogen). It only takes a small dose of THC to disorient the brain.

Most addicts have problems with other drugs, such as alcohol, cocaine, and methamphetamines. Addicts who want to stop taking other drugs will sometimes use marijuana, thinking that it is safer than using other drugs. In some respect that may be true. One may justify it by saying, "I will give up these drugs, but I will keep using marijuana."

Here are some myths and facts:

Myth: Marijuana is pretty harmless.

Fact: Marijuana is extremely potent and poses severe health risks.

Myth: Marijuana is legal in some states and should be legal.

Fact: Marijuana is illegal in all states in America.

Myth: Marijuana gives a pleasant, easy-to-control high.

Fact: Marijuana's effects are very difficult to

predict. It depends on what you smoke and where you get it. Many people have no idea where the drug comes from and who mixed it for them.

Myth: Marijuana is okay to use if you don't use alcohol or cocaine.

Fact: Using marijuana undermines recovery if you are in recovery.

Here is a test. List five other names used to describe marijuana.

1. _____
2. _____
3. _____
4. _____
5. _____

Many of you may ask why you should stop smoking marijuana. Let me be blunt! If you are a weedhead, here are a few reasons why you need to stop.

1. You spend lots of wasted money.
2. You are not allowing your real self to be exposed.
3. You never know where it comes from and what's in it.
4. Your motivation and cognition are always altered.

5. You live in a constant state of paranoia and psychosis.
6. Most often than not, this is the center of your being/life.
7. You cannot truly "live life to the fullest" being high all the time.

Cocaine

I believe crack cocaine is one drug that has damaged more people than any other drug in America. It has crossed almost every economic boundary, to affect the rich, poor, white, black, business, religious — the list continues. You may remember that it has even impacted the lives of some powerful people, like the former mayors of Chicago and Detroit, who were busted for using crack cocaine. There are also many others we did not hear about over the news. This drug is very powerful and destructive. It makes people steal, lie, cheat, sell their bodies, sell their possessions, and even give up their children just to get another hit. Movies have been made, the government has spent countless man hours and enormous amounts of money to combat this drug. Some worked and some did not.

Cocaine is derived from the leaves of the cocoa plant. It is an anesthetic that is often abused as a cerebral stimulus. The newer "freebase," or "crack" cocaine, is a designer drug that is much more potent and now is used by all kinds of people. There is one method that is widely used to produce cocaine. It is made by what's called "kitchen chemists," who mix cocaine with baking soda to produce a yellow-white powder. When heated in a smoking pipe, the pure cocaine vapors rise and, when inhaled, give an intensive high. Some say that this is "better than sex." However, the high only lasts for a few minutes and is often followed by depression and craving for more crack cocaine. The effects for most people include physical and behavioral changes, such as irritability, delusions, and hallucinations, just to name a few.

Cocaine causes damage to the cells in the brain. Those cells, which become damaged, are the same cells that are damaged in people who have Parkinson's disease. By increasing blood level concentrations of certain naturally produced excretions, cocaine increases the heart rate and blood pressure, dilates the pupils, constricts blood vessels, raises the body temperature, and can relax bronchial spasms. Why people do this is beyond me. Chronic cocaine users may gradually deteriorate physically from the lack of sleep, with many users going up to five days without sleeping. Malnutrition and self-neglect happens with chronic users of cocaine, also.

The use of cocaine blocks the coronary arteries, which can no longer supply blood to the heart's pumping muscles. Some people have sudden heart attacks that cause death by cardiac arrest when the heart simply quivers without an effective beat. This has been documented in young people who were very healthy before using cocaine. I am giving you this information because it is my desire to help someone. My intention is to help drug users and their families have a better understanding of what these drugs do and how they affect the mind and body of the user.

Here is a test. List five ways a cocaine user affects the family.

1. _____
2. _____
3. _____
4. _____
5. _____

Here is another test. List five ways that you know people can take cocaine.

1. _____
2. _____
3. _____
4. _____
5. _____

Here is yet another test. List the youngest person you know who has used cocaine.

Age: _____ Male _____ Female _____

Many may ask why they should stop smoking

cocaine. Let me be blunt again. If you are a cokehead, here are a few reasons why you need to stop.

You could die.

1. You lose your identity and will lie, steal, and do whatever it takes to get high, even if it involves selling your body or hurting someone else.
2. You are ingesting all type of dangerous chemicals and volatile solvents.
3. You become very unhealthy (a terrible way to lose weight).
4. You really hurt the people who care and love you.
5. You will never live life to the fullest while using this drug.

CHAPTER IV

DESTROYING OTHERS

39. IT'S TIME TO STOP: Being In Everyone's Business.
40. IT'S TIME TO STOP: Being Mean To Others.
41. IT'S TIME TO STOP: Cheating Each Other.
42. IT'S TIME TO STOP: Creating Misery For Others.
43. IT'S TIME TO STOP: Having Unwanted Children.
44. IT'S TIME TO STOP: Hurting Animals.
45. IT'S TIME TO STOP: Hurting The Planet.
46. IT'S TIME TO STOP: Killing Trees.
47. IT'S TIME TO STOP: Lying To Each Other.
48. IT'S TIME TO STOP: Playing With Other People's Minds.
49. IT'S TIME TO STOP: War.

CHAPTER V

I CAN'T HELP MYSELF

50. IT'S TIME TO STOP: Asking Others For Help, But Not Helping Yourself.
51. IT'S TIME TO STOP: Begging.
52. IT'S TIME TO STOP: Being Sad.
53. IT'S TIME TO STOP: **Being Scared Of Yourself.**

Stop terrorizing yourself with your thoughts. It is a very bad way to live life. Take the time and find a mental picture that gives you happiness. Right away you will change your scary thoughts to good thoughts. Your life is important. Believe it and do something about it now! Life is too short for you to be scared of yourself.

54. IT'S TIME TO STOP: Being Stupid.
55. IT'S TIME TO STOP: Being The Victim.
56. IT'S TIME TO STOP: Doubting Yourself.

57. IT'S TIME TO STOP: Hoping.
58. IT'S TIME TO STOP: **Just Being A Damn Idiot.** Just stop! You know what you are doing, and you know that sometimes you can just be out of control. You have seen others looking at you. Put your mind to what you are doing. Take your time. And, believe me, everything you desire is going to work out. You know you are talented. You know you are smart. Most importantly, you know you can do anything you set your mind to if you just stop being a damn idiot.
59. IT'S TIME TO STOP: Treating Yourself As A Victim.
60. IT'S TIME TO STOP: Walking Around In A Daze.
61. IT'S TIME TO STOP: Wasting Money.
62. IT'S TIME TO STOP: **Seeing Yourself As Being Unwanted.**

You may think you do not belong anywhere—whether you are at work, at home, with your family, or with associates. You must understand that as long as you are breathing, you have a place in life. You are here, and you have to deal with it. When you see that you matter and you are of substance, you will accept the fact that the people who make you feel unwanted may not be the people you should associate with. It's Time To Stop!

Sometimes we may feel we are not supported or encouraged, and we take on the feeling of being unwanted. Many times when we are misunderstood and not accepted, we can feel unwanted. It is a fact that we are often treated as being unjustified and unsubstantiated. We may have taught people to treat us the way we are treated. Let me explain. Sometimes we go unheard because we were silent when we could have spoken up. It may have been a parent or a person whom we highly respect that we chose not to say what should have been stated at the time, leaving that other person to make their own opinion about a certain situation. When a person asks our opinions, most of us agree and just go along with the other person's opinions, when we could have stated our purposes or thoughts. There are many who never want to make the boat tip; some do not want to make waves, and others do not want to make anyone upset.

There comes a time when you must speak out. You have to tell others what's on your mind and inform others of your likes and dislikes. You must state your case. Yes, someone may not agree, and maybe even someone will become upset. When you tell someone how you feel, it lets the other person know where you stand. Many times, even in a heated battle, when you are expressive and not silent, the other person is aware of your thoughts. You are never wrong until you believe that you are or someone informs you that you are.

Your life means a great deal to you, as well as to someone else. You need to see that you have a place in this life and that you affect someone else, whether in a positive or negative manner. The most important idea is to know that you are very important. Remember that you can make a positive statement/impact to a younger person who you may not realize is watching you and wanting to be just like you. That young person is watching your actions, the life that you lead, and how you deal with situations that come into your life.

The Universal Source/Creator wants you to see life as a good thing. You must change the way you feel about yourself. Love yourself in spite of what others may think or say about you. Here are a few steps to encourage you.

1. Say to yourself everyday that you are loved.
2. Know that you are wanted and needed.
3. Accept who you are and be proud of it.
4. Never be ashamed of who you are.
5. Know that your inputs always matter.
6. You can live life to the fullest.

These six steps can help others to accept who you are and, at the very least, help you to become respected for your thoughts. You are always in control of not surrounding yourself or associating yourself where you are unwanted. Wherever you are in this life, whatever position you hold, you have it. You are here at this moment; you are learning or teaching someone else. So stop thinking that you are unwanted. Someone needs and wants you, whether you believe it or not.

CHAPTER VI

SEEING THE WORST

63. IT'S TIME TO STOP: **Denying Life.**

Everyday life begins, and life ends. Everyday a baby is born, and an elder dies. Flowers bloom, and others wilt and die. Someone gets hired, and another person gets fired. A happy couple gets married, and an unhappy couple gets divorced. Someone buys a home, and a family's home gets foreclosed. Some lucky guy purchases a shiny new car, and someone else's old car breaks down.

Sometimes in our lives, there is nothing that we can do but go with the flow. We do not, nor can we ever, control what comes to us. But, we can impact life. And we do control the things that come *from* us. We cannot stop the things that come into our lives. People are living as if life is not a real entity, that they are somehow invincible, that they cannot be touched, that as long as they stay in their corner of life they will be secure, that nothing will touch them. Come out of denial!

Why are you stopping the process of life for yourself and your family? If you want nothing for your life, that's fine. Stop the process of denying others the opportunity. Have you stopped to think why you are afraid of life? What makes you always stop before the finish line? What makes you stay in the same old rut, knowing that you really do not have to? How many times have you started something and never completed it? Wake Up! It's time to stop denying life.

64. IT'S TIME TO STOP: Living Life As A Joke.
65. IT'S TIME TO STOP: Looking For The Worst In Everything.
66. IT'S TIME TO STOP: Seeing The World As Only A Bad Place.
67. IT'S TIME TO STOP: Seeing The Worst In Yourself.
68. IT'S TIME TO STOP: **Seeing The Worst In Others.**

Seeing the worst in others may represent your low self-esteem. You are whole and worthy of having the best that life has to offer. Every person who enters your space, whether it's for a long or short period of time, is there for a purpose. You are also in their space to teach them as they may be teaching you. You cannot see the worst in everyone.

IT'S TIME TO STOP

You have two choices. You can choose to remove them from your space or to remove yourself from the situation. Before you decide to remove a long time friend, co-worker, or possibly be a family member, try to take a moment to understand that person's needs, wants, desires, and personality. You may find out where all the negative energy comes from and be better able to deal with that person. Before you pass judgment, look for the best in someone. Take time to notice the little things that are unique about that person. Try to find out what makes that person tick. Again, this may help you to find the good in someone whom you thought was all bad. In time, if you can't find any positive energy in that person, remember that you have control of your life. Your space is important, and you are to preserve that space at any cost by not allowing anything to devour its walls. Start looking for the good, not just in people, but everything that comes into your life. Enjoy your time and space. You deserve the best. It's time to stop seeing the worst in others.

CHAPTER VII

LOSING CONTROL

68. IT'S TIME TO STOP: Allowing Others To Do For You.
69. IT'S TIME TO STOP: Being A Follower And Not Thinking Independently.
70. IT'S TIME TO STOP: Being So Damn Lazy.
71. IT'S TIME TO STOP: Being Unmotivated.
72. IT'S TIME TO STOP: Wishing The World Would Come To An End.
73. IT'S TIME TO STOP: Believing That Someone Owes You Something.
74. IT'S TIME TO STOP: **Not Taking Responsibility.**

Responsibility can be a huge word for some people. Responsibility can also be frightening. Responsibility can be defined as taking ownership; a duty or an obligation. Every now and then we all go through a period in our lives of being irresponsible. We also know that it will catch up with us, sometimes when we don't want it to.

As children, we are taught to be responsible for our toys by putting them up when we were done playing with them, cleaning our rooms, taking a complete bath (Don't forget behind the ears.), feeding the pets, washing the dishes, and cleaning the yard. As we grow, we are taught to be responsible for ourselves and others. When we become older, we **must be responsible.** Taking responsibility is taking ownership of what you say you will do. Being responsible is simply this: If you have it, you take care of it. Yes, it's just that simple.

Let's get down to it.
- If you have children, take responsibility for them.
- If you have a job, be responsible, and do the job well.
- If you are married or have a significant other, be responsible in your relationship.
- If you have bills, take responsibility, and pay off your commitments on time or as soon as possible. It will cost you less in the long run.
- If you are renting or buying a home, be responsible because it's where YOU live.
- If you are considered to be someone's best friend, do what it takes to be a best friend.
- If you do wrong, take responsibility for your actions, and correct your issues.

- If you are in any leadership role, take responsibility seriously, and treat people as people and not machines.
- If you are a sister/brother, aunt/uncle, mother/father, or grandparent, take responsibility, and be just that. Sometimes it may hurt to tell the truth, but that's what family members are for. It is your responsibility to love, and, sometimes, love hurts. Overall, be responsible, and take great care of your loved ones. You get the picture.

For whatever you have and in whatever you do, you must be responsible. You will know that you have matured when you begin to take ownership of what is around you. You will know that you have matured when you stop making foolish mistakes and change your way of thinking. You will be able to enjoy life more abundantly when you become more responsible. You will see your life turn around. You have no reason to be afraid. When you take responsibility for your life, you will gain the confidence to continue to succeed and be prosperous with everything that you do. It's time to stop and be responsible.

75. IT'S TIME TO STOP: Giving Up.
76. IT'S TIME TO STOP: **Living With Your Parents.**

Take care of yourself! I know that times are hard, and, believe me, I know how hard it is to have money to take care of yourself. I know what it means to be in school or without a job. But if you are over thirty years of age, it's time to stop living with your parents.

You may have very cool and understanding parents who may never want you to leave. Believe me, I know what it's like to always have fresh clothing, home cooked meals, a clean room, and not too many worries but your own house. There comes a time in everyone's life when they need to be independent. For some of you that may be a bad word, but independence is actually a good thing. It builds character, self-esteem, pride, and, most importantly, self-worth. Yes, it's a scary, big world out there, but you are not alone in that sentiment. Here is a quote I enjoy: "When I was a child, I did think like a child. But now that I am an adult, I must behave like I have some sense." —Stan

Now, there is nothing about living with our parents when we fall on hard times. I'm really not speaking to you unless you are one of the ones who have been there for more than two years. It's Time To Stop Living With Your Parents. It is a very different thing if your parents are living with you for health or safety reasons.

You should also move out if you are raising children. It becomes very difficult to raise children in an environment that is overcrowded. It makes it hard to motivate your children to do the things that you wish for them. You may say that your parents are good parents and that you turned out very well.

Yes, you may be correct, but they should not be raising you and your kids at their house. Grandma and grandpa are special, loving, and caring people, but you must remember that they are grandparents. They are supposed to be grandparents who baby-sit for a few hours, maybe even a few days, and then the grandchildren go back to the parents. They had their turn raising children. They raised you. Now, get out of their house, and find a place to raise them your own. Your parents should be allowed to spend their golden years in peace, in joy of being grandparents, and, most importantly, without the worry of keeping house for you and your family. Need I go on?

Many of you may not have children and still live with your parents. Go ahead and take the plunge. Go out and explore this big, scary world. You will find that it is not that scary. If you spend time seeing the lay of the land, you will find that it is not that big. It is time to stop living with your parents, now!

77. IT'S TIME TO STOP: Waiting For Others To Do Something First.
78. IT'S TIME TO STOP: Wanting Something For Nothing.

CHAPTER VIII

FOR THE GENERATIONS

79. IT'S TIME TO STOP: Being A Deadbeat Parent/Person.
80. IT'S TIME TO STOP: Believing That You Must Be Married.
81. IT'S TIME TO STOP: Believing That You Must Have Children.
82. IT'S TIME TO STOP: Consenting To Bad Education For Your Children.
83. IT'S TIME TO STOP: Living In The Past.
84. IT'S TIME TO STOP: **Not Listening To Your Children.**

Do children have anything to say? Do children have a voice? Do your children listen to you? The answers to these questions will almost always be the same: "Of course not." Most of us adults can say that at one time or another when we were children, we did not listen to our parents. We wanted to do our own thing. Most of us felt that our parents did not know what was going on in our worlds. They were from the old school, were outdated, and just wanted to be in our business. You may have said that the times changed, and the way they did things was not the way you wanted to do things.

Back then and now, just as it has always been, listening to our parents is very important. Communication, or the lack thereof, has broken families apart. It has driven children to run away and to experiment with drugs. Parents today must know that listening is a must-needed parental skill.

Take this test. Write down five reasons why you think some parents do not listen to their children.

1. _____
2. _____
3. _____
4. _____
5. _____

Not listening to our children can send the wrong messages. Everyone needs someone who listens. However, if we could hear what we tell others, it's a wonder why anyone would listen to us. We can come up with some wacky stuff.

As adults, we have friends, co-workers, family, educators, neighbors, and clergy who are available to lend an ear. Most of us have someone we can turn to to listen to the stuff that comes out of our mouths. Why would we think that children don't know what they are saying? Some of us parents may feel the people listening to our children are people we don't approve of. It is vital that we, as parents, take time to listen to our children. If our children come home and say that adults are mistreating them, even if they are relatives, we should take note. If they are telling us that teachers don't like them and always pick on them, we should not push our children away and say, "How could your teachers not like you?" Not all teachers get along with all students. *(No offense to teachers).*

If our children tell us that adults touched them in an inappropriate manner, do not push them away. Take stock and listen. Not too many kids will say something like that just for the heck of it. Yes, many may want attention, and many will do anything to get it, but if we have healthy relationships with our children, we will never hear anything like our children telling us that they were touched by adults unless it is true. We have all seen what has happened in the last couple of years with people coming out to say that they were molested when they were children. Many were afraid that no one would believe them, so they kept it as a secret.

As bizarre as it may seem, children would love for their parents to listen to them. Most have tried since birth to get their parents to listen. But, like many of us, they hear some of the same things we heard our parents say to us, like "Get out of here;" "I don't want to hear that;" "You don't know what you are talking about;" and, "Go to your room." If you have heard sayings like this or others, you remember how you felt when you were trying to tell your parents something. Well, it's the same if you express the same sentiments to your children. They feel the same as you did when you heard those words.

Today, many parents work from home and home school their children at the same time. Envision this scenario. You are working on a project for work with a deadline that is fast approaching. Your child walks up to you and just starts talking. Because you are really busy at the moment, you hear your child grabbling about something, but you do not understand them. You briefly stop what you are doing to look at your child, but you keep working. Your child continues talking. Out of frustration, you say, "I hear you, baby. I understand, son. Give me a minute, and I will talk to you later. I'm busy at the moment." What do you think your child is thinking? Some may just let it go, but others may think that you are always too busy to talk to them.

Stop and take note that there are companies and business that will take advantage of your child's propensity and need to talk to someone. The cellular companies are making billions of dollars each year from people constantly listening and talking to each other. Many companies target the younger generation because they know that children have lots to say. They can talk for hours, just like we did it when we were younger. You will know what I'm talking about when you see your cell phone bill.

It's time to start listening to our children. Our children deserve our undivided attention. They are growing up in a world that has so much information that is right and wrong. They need direction, and who better to give it to them than their parents who love and care for them. If you will not, believe this, someone else will.

Our children need more than just an ear from us. They need our total concentration. We can learn as much from them as they can learn from us. As the world changes, we can learn how it is changing from our children; they are the ones who are contributing to that change. Want to know what a rap song is saying? (I sure can't understand it.) Ask your child to explain it to you. You maybe be astonished by what you hear. Do you want to know what your child thinks about love? Again, ask. You may be surprised by what they already know. Take the time not just to hear what your child is saying—truly listen. Remember that listening is taking the time to fully understand what another is saying. When a child cries for the first time, parents are in tune to those cries. They understand what those cries and tears mean. As your children become older, why is it that we stop being tuned in when they learned how to talk and are better able to communicate with us?

Below are three steps that will help you to listen and communicate with your children.

Look at your child in his/her eyes. It is extremely important that you make eye contact with your child. Looking at your child will demonstrate to them that you are concentrating on what they are saying. Your body language and facial expressions will also demonstrate to your child that you are listening.

#

Do not interrupt your child, even if you know the answer or have heard that story before. Give them time to get out what they are trying to say. Many of us will interrupt others when we have a comment, or we do not want to forget a thought. Most children don't forget; they just have a hard time processing thoughts. It may take them longer to express themselves.

#

Stop whatever you are doing at that moment. If you need to talk to them at another time, be pleasant about it. Make sure that keep your promise that you will discuss it with them later. Never allow too much time to pass without talking with your child. It may not be important to you, but you can bet that it is important to them. You may be surprised at the response you receive from your child.

The best relationship is one that has effective communication. Stop and listen to your child. It may just save their lives.

CHAPTER IX

WHO ME?

85. IT'S TIME TO STOP: Allowing Your Ego To Control Your Life.
86. IT'S TIME TO STOP: Being So Jealous.
87. IT'S TIME TO STOP: **Being The One Who Always Gets Things Started.**

You just need to stop and allow someone else to do things before you put your two cents in. You may never know. It may be time for a change. Everyone deserves a chance to be a leader. I do agree that there are times when we all feel that if we don't do it, it will not be done. That may be the time when we need to change the people we surround ourselves with. I'm not advocating that the people we surround ourselves with are not capable, but there comes a time when we need others' input or participation into a situation or idea. Just stop and give someone else a chance.

88. IT'S TIME TO STOP: **Being Ungrateful.**

So often, we all become ungrateful for the things that are going on within our lives because of the many pressures we face each day. Most of us face pressures to complete, compete, to be correct, to be first, to finish, to create, to be perfect, to be on time, to deliver, to be what others deem to be right, and to have more and to produce, just to name a few. In those times, we often forget to take the time to appreciate what we have and what we do not have. This leads us to becoming ungrateful. It's time to stop and take time to be grateful.

If we would take the time to look at what we have, we would be more grateful. There are myriad reasons why we should do this. The major thing I find myself appreciating is the fact that there are so many people who do not have what I have. In some respects it is good, but in other respects, I do not have what others have. In this I mean the good things and the bad things. Let me explain. I have been following Oprah for a few years. I'm happy that I do not have what she has. Oprah has a huge amount of money, but along with all of her success and riches, she also has an enormous amount of pressure.

Here are a few things that you can start taking a look at every day of your life to become grateful. Remember that what you have could be gone in a flash. When you are grateful, you are positioning yourself to receive more. It is known that many believe if they had more than they do, they would not appreciate the more. I believe that when you can appreciate what you have, and really appreciate it, you are more than able to appreciate the more.

1. If you are in good health, that's enough to be grateful.
2. If you have a car, maybe not the best, but a car, and it's paid for, that's enough to be grateful.
3. If you have family that loves, respects, and supports each other, that's enough for you to be grateful.
4. If you have a little money, or just enough to pay bills on time, that's enough to be grateful.
5. If you have employment (any kind) — we all know what the job market is like — that's enough to be grateful.
6. If you have a roof over your head, maybe not be the roof that you would like, but it's there for you at this moment — while many others are living on streets — that's enough to be grateful.
7. If you have your own thought pattern, and you can make decisions for yourself, that's enough to be grateful.

The list can go on and on. Make a list for yourself. List things that are in your life that you can be grateful for. Look at them every day. Place them inside your heart. Memorize them. It will help you to be grateful.

As stated many times throughout this book, we do not have control of what comes to us, but we do have control of what comes *from* us. Thanking the Creator every day keeps you in the spirit of being grateful.

Take a moment each day (in the morning before you start your day) to just say "thanks." It has been proven that there is something much greater than we are. That's a topic for another book. But that something, whatever you choose to call it, deserves the respect of your gratefulness. Being in a state of gratitude will keep you grounded to receive more of your hearts desire, as well as needs. It's time to stop being ungrateful.

89. IT'S TIME TO STOP: Being What Others Want You To Be.
90. IT'S TIME TO STOP: Believing That You Know What Is Best For Others.
91. IT'S TIME TO STOP: **Criticizing.**

Criticizing never changes a darn thing. It's time to stop criticizing yourself. Accept yourself exactly as you are. When you criticize yourself, your changes are usually negative. When you approve of yourself, your changes are usually positive.

92. IT'S TIME TO STOP: **Procrastinating.**

Tomorrow is not promised to anyone. Most have heard the saying "Never put off tomorrow what you can do today." Yes, there are always some things that can wait until tomorrow. But, delaying dreams cannot be a part of waiting, going to school, or learning to drive, beginning a new project, learning a new language, being a better person, loving more, giving more of yourself, and helping others. Procrastinating can slow a project and hinder its efforts. Procrastinating can cost you time and money. If you are a procrastinator, you understand what I mean. We all have a little procrastinator in us, oftentimes it can be a defense mechanism, for others it's just laziness. We all know that nothing can ever be complete or successful if we procrastinate. It's Time to Stop.

93. IT'S TIME TO STOP: Hating The Player.
94. IT'S TIME TO STOP: Hating The Game.
95. IT'S TIME TO STOP: Taking Yourself So Damn Seriously.
96. IT'S TIME TO STOP: Thinking That Everyone Else Is An Idiot.
97. IT'S TIME TO STOP: Thinking That Everyone Else Is Out To Hurt You.
98. IT'S TIME TO STOP: **Thinking That You Can't Do Anything Wrong.**
    You are not perfect. I know that you want to believe that you are, but I'll let you on a little secret. The only one who is perfect is the Creator.
99. IT'S TIME TO STOP: Thinking You Are Perfect.

100. **IT'S TIME TO STOP! Start Living Each Day As Best As Possible.**

Take the time to stop and see what this life is all about. You will come to this weird conclusion that it is not all that bad. It is about you and a great deal more. Each day you are alive is one of the greatest gifts that you can have. Live each day by keeping an open mind. You should make it another day remember to be grateful for what you have at that moment. Remember that whatever you have, or whatever you are going through, someone else is going through it, too. They may not have as much as you have, and they may be into something just a little deeper than you could ever imagine. Most things that go on in our lives that we do not appreciate or want are things that we created. At best, they would go in a much different direction if we took the time to stop and look at them.

Poor illness is sometimes caused by our inability to listen to our bodies. When our bodies give us the warning signs that something is not right, most of us just ignore them and believe that they will go away. Yes, sometimes they do, but other times we need to take a position, and stop, and maybe see a specialist, see a doctor, or even slow down from our busy lives. My point is that each of us must take time and become aware of our surroundings. As we grow older, our bodies, minds, and souls begin to follow that path.

WHO ME?

The things that we were accustomed to we often do not do anymore; and, sometimes, we really do not want to do them anyway. As we grow older, we must learn from the past, stopping to smell the roses, smell the water and, most importantly, smell life.

Life is real. Everything that makes your life what it is, you have something that you can do about it. You can make the changes you desire. You can make those desires a reality if you stop and look at them, stop and appreciate them, stop and see them for what they are. You may see life as an individual journey, but you must understand that you must include others. You did not get here by yourself; you needed a male and a female. You needed someone to help you to learn how to talk, to walk, to read, to appreciate or not, to validate or not. I'm saying that you needed someone throughout your entire life. Now it's your turn to help someone else. Someone is watching you. It does not matter what way you think your life is, whether it's good or bad, someone wants to be just like you. Someone wants to have your strength, your courage, your wit, your graciousness, your money, and your home.

You, as an individual, must take pride in what you are. If you are just a fifteen-year-old teenager, there is someone who is ten years old who wants to be just like you. The same goes for someone who is forty years of age. Someone is watching you and wants to be just like you. What are you doing in your life that affects someone else in a positive manner? The older we become, the more aware we are to become. At the very moment that you understand that statement, you will begin to see what life is all about.

Have fun along the way at whatever you are doing and/or want to do. The more you do it, the more you will enjoy what you do. I can guarantee that you will not want to STOP.

> "BE GOOD TO YOURSELF
> AND SOMEONE ELSE."

IT'S TIME TO STOP

ANSWERS TO EXERCISES/QUESTIONS

6. **IT'S TIME TO STOP:** Not Knowing Who You Are.

Three Minute Test

If you have completed all of the lines within the three minute period, you can say that you know **Who You Are**. Take time to review each of your answers and become more familiar and know what they really mean. You may change or add a few as needed. Review your list again. If you listed only positive things about yourself, and did not list any negatives, you need to reevaluate yourself. You have things about you that are unpleasant. You must understand that those things about you that you think are unpleasant are really not that bad. For example, if you did not list that you are a "nosey/curious" person, and you know that you are sometimes bothered by that, it doesn't mean that you are a bad person. You may just be a person who needs/wants to know the facts about everything. In some instances, that could be a great thing.

If you listed that you get angry over things that really do not matter, it could mean that you do not take the time to think things over, or you may want things to go your way all the time. Your negatives are you. It makes your weak attributes strong. It is important that you know your negatives, and you understand and accept them as a part of **Who You Are**: How they can and do affect your daily life and how you can possibly live a little happier with yourself and others. No one is a perfect person. No one can ever do everything right. You must accept **Who You Are** and become in love with who you are. You have to make the best of **Who You Are** and learn to live life to the fullest. "Be good to yourself and remember to be good to others."

If you did not complete the entire list, take time to reevaluate yourself, and take time each day to become familiar with yourself. It's okay to go to dinner alone, to go to the movies alone, or to take a short trip alone. It takes time to get to know yourself. Take the time to listen to your body and become in love with **Who You Are.**

27. IT'S TIME TO STOP: Drinking So Much:

ANSWERS TO EXERCISES/QUESTIONS

List five things that you believe are complications and symptoms of alcohol abuse.
1. Depressant
2. Mood swings
3. Loner
4. Negative personal appearance and responsibilities
5. Impaired coordination

List five things that alcohol does for a person.
1. Metabolizes the liver / *Relaxation*
2. Depressant to the central nervous system/ *Relaxation*
3. Depresses brain cells/ *Feel Sad*
4. Enables one to feel numb/ *Alters ones thinking/moods*
5. Inhibits ones equilibrium/ *Happy/Escape*

Italics = another way of answering this test

List five things that a person uses while consuming alcohol.
1. Use drugs
2. Smoke cigarettes
3. Eat food
4. Aspirin for hangovers
5. Prescription drugs

38. IT'S TIME TO STOP: Using Drugs That Control

IT'S TIME TO STOP

Your Mind:
List five other names used to describe marijuana.
1. Hemp
2. Weed
3. Pot
4. Ganja
5. Grass

List five ways a cocaine user affects the family.
1. Emotionally
2. Confusion
3. Dishonesty
4. Abuse
5. Financially

List five ways that you know cocaine can be taken.
1. Orally
2. Snorting
3. Smoking
4. Intravenously/IV
5. Eating/Chewing through foods, etc.

84. IT'S TIME TO STOP: Not Listening To Your Children.
List five reasons why you think some parents do not listen to their children.
1. Too busy
2. Don't care

ANSWERS TO EXERCISES/QUESTIONS

3. Have other children who need their attention
4. Cannot understand what their children need
5. They may be a child themselves

STANLEY W. ALLEN has devoted over twenty years to counseling people and helping them to live their lives to the fullest. This is his first published work with many more to come. He currently lives in Texas.

Register online at www.carmaapublishing.com for more information on this and other great books.